Federico Illesi

Gin & Tonic

the history and recipes of a perfect cocktail

pensieriparole

First published: December 2023

ISBN: 978-88-31206-26-6

Original title: Gin & Tonic, Storia e ricette di un cocktail perfetto

Translated by Jacquelyn White

Via Don Giovanni Verità, 14
35131 – Padova
Web: edizioni.pensieriparole.it

Cover and back cover photograph by Mihail Iosip
www.mihailiosip.com

"The gin and tonic has saved more Englishmen's lives, and minds, than all the doctors in the Empire".

—Sir Winston Churchill

PREFACE

Years of experiments and attempts, on my own and with complicit friends, have led to writing this book, which aims to be a simple account, without excessive digressions, of the creation of the gin and tonic up to the present day.

Not merely a history of "Gin and Tonic", but also a series of gin cocktail recipes along with my top tips, fruit of over ten years' experience in the sector.

A journey which started, as for many, by randomly mixing a few ingredients, such as gin with tonic, rum with coke or vodka with lemon soda, to then try to grow and evolve with the flavors, navigating the boundless art of mixology, always driven by curiosity.

Testing new cocktails, experimenting new flavors, in some cases trying recipes handed down over centuries, I gradually expanded my horizons. A good method, especially when travelling abroad, is to order signature cocktails to become familiar with the trends and typical tastes of the place.

Reaching the pinnacle of this journey, which starts with what is considered the base (gin/tonic) and then is enhanced by mixing other products such as vermouth, liquors or spirits, wines, fruit juices, bitters, to return once again to removing superfluous elements, arriving at purity, at the essential, at a new point of balance. This is how I rediscovered the Gin & Tonic: the perfect cocktail.

INTRODUCTION

The book essentially consists of five parts: the first part illustrates the journey of gin and tonic from its discovery, to near-disappearance and then revival, up to the boom we observe today. Its history is punctuated by trivia and little anecdotes that might come in handy for you to engage in a good conversation or to impress your dinner companions.

The information reported is credited by several books, but as it happens in such cases, certain facts may actually be the result of legends passed down and told and retold, so much so they are now unanimously regarded as truth.

The second part is devoted to methods of making gin, with the addition of some regulatory aspects for those who might want to try their hand at making this alcohol.

The third part, on the other hand, celebrates the preparation of the Gin & Tonic, analyzed in every step, from the choice of the glass to that of the ice, from the equipment required to the more or less useful garnishes.

The fourth part presents ten alternatives to the classic Gin & Tonic and, finally, the last one with thirty recipes that you can also prepare at home to impress your guests during a cocktail party or dinner, with doses, ingredients and suggestions for the best composition of your drink.

CHAPTER I
The history of a legend

Contrary to what one might think, at the origins of gin lies an extraordinary experimentation by some Benedictine monks under the influence of the Salerno Medical School in the 11th century. The "Compendium Salernitanum" of 1055 describes a distillation of wine, infused with juniper berries gathered in large quantities on the hills near Salerno.

The origins of gin would thus have its roots on Italian soil, although the researchers' goal was not to create an alcoholic beverage, but rather to preserve and spread the medicinal benefits of juniper, whose properties had already been observed in ancient Egypt, where the berries were successfully used for embalming.

The monks took “aqua vitae” and began to add juniper berries, whose virtues had already been described by Pliny the Elder in Naturalis Historia (77-79 AD): «[Juniper] is prescribed for convulsions, ruptures, griping pains in the bowels, affections of the uterus, and sciatica, either in a dose of four berries in white wine, or in the form of a decoction of twenty berries in wine».

Around the mid-1200s Pope John XXI, in his treatise on eye care, the Liber de Oculo, mentioned another ancestor of gin, prepared with various "botanicals," referred to as "eye water". He asserted it prolongs good health, dispels superfluous moods, revives the heart and keeps people young.

The first actual description of gin dates back to the Antwerp-based physician Philippus Hermanni, who mentioned a distilled beverage flavored with juniper in his 1552 book Een Constelijck Distileerboec.

In 1650 pharmacist and physician Sylvius Franciscus, a former professor at the University of Leiden, found a remedy for stomach and kidney ailments using juniper infused in grain alcohol. A medicinal "potion" capable of releasing the beneficial effects of juniper berries, with antiseptic power for the blood. The diuretic properties of the berries have the power to combat gout: an accumulation of uric acids due to an unbalanced diet rich in meat, once very common among the wealthier social classes in Holland. Gin, in fact, is not a distillation of juniper; rather the berries are used to flavor the alcohol, which is subsequently and further distilled to make a clear, balsamic product. The emergence of gin in this small part of Europe was fostered by the large merchant fleet and the Dutch East Indies Company, which was founded here in 1602. Jenever was even called Dutch Courage, so much so that it was adopted by English troops during wartime operations in the Thirty Years' War.

During the same period, Spanish settlers discovered that the natives used the bark of the Cinchona tree to cure fever: a miraculous plant that the Jesuits spread throughout Europe to cure the plague.

In 1736, the English discovered the properties of the bark and realized that it was also very effective against malaria. The quinine "tonic" soon spread throughout the world: it was the dawn of the Gin and Tonic.

Although other beverages were available, it was precisely gin (which became commonly used among the British working class at that time) that caused concern because of its high consumption. Even in the eighteenth century, a portion of British workers' wages was paid in gin. This custom led to a number of problems, especially social ones, including an increase in the spread of alcoholism.

Between 1729 and 1751, in order to limit the consumption of gin, five laws were enacted in Britain known as the Gin Act. These laws restricted mixing and imposed a high taxation on the drink, so much so that its popularity was reduced in favor of cheaper ones including tea. These measures, whose purpose was to restrict the production and consumption of Geneva, did not achieve the hoped-for results and were only temporary, as we shall see in America during the prohibition years and in England, where production and consumption initially suffered a setback. Instead, the measure favored clandestine production and gave a boost to imports from France and Holland, particularly from the town of Schiedam, the name by which the English still identify Dutch gin today.

The "Gin Act" did not achieve its purpose, but it was not futile. In fact, after its repeal, when gin was subject to fiscal control, it contributed to creating competition among the various producers, resulting in an increase in the quality of the marketed product.

In 1794, the German chemist, Johann Jacob Schweppe created soda as a medicine. The primitive tonic water was combined with sweetener and carbon dioxide to make it more palatable and pleasant for patients. In the 18th century, when the British colonized India, they brought gin and tonic with them. The two ingredients were soon also enriched by lime, a citrus fruit known for its anti-inflammatory, antiseptic, and bactericidal properties.

Since the 1800s, the Gin & Tonic has evolved and changed form. A change that occurred thanks to the courage of large and small (sometimes micro) distilleries, which without forgetting juniper (a key ingredient), experimented with the use of new botanicals and flavors. On the other hand, the years to come would witness the emergence of the first mixologists, who would begin to experiment and serve new drinks.

In 1806 the word "cocktail" first appeared, defined by a U.S. newspaper in Hudson, New York as: "a stimulating liquor, composed of spirits of any kind, sugar, water, and bitters··· capable to be an excellent potion as it renders the heart bold and fuddles the mind."

According to legend, the word "cocktail" is derived from the union of the English words "cock" and "tail," perhaps because as early as the 1400s, a colorful drink inspired by the colors of the fighting rooster's tail was drunk in the English countryside.

The milestone in the world of mixologists seems to be represented by Harry Johnson, a San Francisco bartender, in 1860 with the first publication in the cocktail world called the "Bartender Manual," in which vermouth and gin-based drinks are found, the most famous of which was certainly the Martinez, a cocktail consisting of 45 ml of London Dry Gin, 45 ml of red vermouth, a bar spoon of Maraschino and two dashes of Orange Bitter.

Instead, 1862 is the year of "The Bartender's Guide," the first and true guide in the history of drinks, written by Professor Jerry Thomas, considered the father of the art of mixing cocktails. In addition to writing the first drink book ever published, the creativity and spectacular nature of his work defined and codified the image of the bartender as a creative professional.

Thomas updated the book several times until 1876 and it has been reprinted until today with the title “The Bon-Vivant’s Companion".

The drinks covered were sour-basic mixtures such as the "Sour," which thus gave rise to the controversial history of the Tom and John Collin's, but also the Mandarin Punch, the sovereign king of drinks at the time, and the Mint Julep (made with mint and Bourbon-type whiskey), defined as the ancestor of the Mojito.

THREE HISTORIC EVENTS TO REMEMBER

In parallel between America and Europe, three defining historical moments changed the way the inhabitants of the entire planet drank: phylloxera, the availability of crystalline ice, and the invention of the shaker.

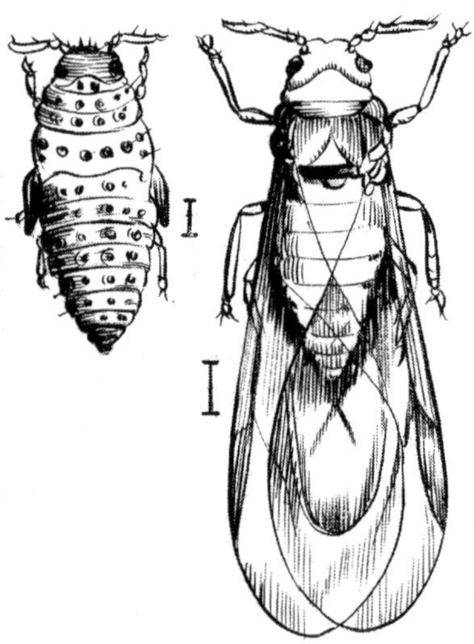

In the second half of the 19th century, a small insect native to North America appeared in Europe - the phylloxera (Viteus vitifoliae), a powerful pest that literally devastated entire vineyards across the continent. The direct effect of phylloxera on the cocktail world was the disappearance of brandy, cognac and all vermouth-based drinks (all grape derivatives) from European drink lists. These drinks continued to be served only in the most prestigious establishments.

The Sazerac cocktail was modified with Bourbon and people began to make more use of local spirits including gin.

Cocktails became much drier and the vermouth parts, which were generally used as a base for drinks, were replaced with distillate or in some cases used sparingly as a "two dashes of..." flavoring.

In the same years, another event determined the diffusion of cocktails as we know them today: the availability of crystalline ice.

John Gorrie together with Federic Tudor, a powerful businessman of the time, began to market huge blocks of ice from the pure waters of America's countless frozen lakes.

The huge crystalline blocks were sawn and subsequently loaded into merchant ships inside barrels thermally insulated with straw and cloths, and then sold to locals and wealthier people in neighboring states.

The seasonal voyages proved to be a real success, so much so that for the first time in history the ice arrived still intact in Martinique.

Tudor was nicknamed "Ice Man." The title was bestowed on him when ships with 180 tons of ice left America and arrived in Calcutta after four months at sea: the remaining 100 tons still intact were sold to the powerful people of India at exorbitant prices.

Word spread around the world, attracting the attention of Thaddeus Lowe, an intellectual and scientist, largely self-taught in chemistry, meteorology and aeronautics. During his lifetime, he engaged in a wide range of activities, including the production of hydrogen gas, the construction of hot-air balloons and the invention and patenting of ice machines and the use of refrigerated ships for transportation. Thus began the era of ... "on the rocks".

All the respectable bars of the time, even in Europe, could not wait to buy the infamous contraption, as was the case in Italy as well: it was precisely in those years that the two greatest cocktails on the rocks in the history of the Bel Paese were born: the Americano and the Negroni.

The creation of the Americano dates back to 1860, at the Bar Gaspare Campari in Milan, as a variation of the Milano-Torino cocktail (MITO), much loved by American tourists, who were in the habit of requesting the addition of soda.

In the 1920s, Count Camillo Negroni was a regular at the aristocratic Caffè Casoni in via de' Tornabuoni in Florence and, to vary from his usual aperitif Americano, he asked the bartender Fosco Scarselli to add some gin in place of seltzer, in honor of his last trips to London. The new cocktail became known as the "Americano Count Negroni-style"- that is, an Americano with gin added - and was later named after the count himself.

The third event is the creation of the shaker: in early 1871, William Hernett applied to the New York patent office for a license to manufacture an instrument to be used for mixing drinks. The Franklin D. Roosevelt Presidential Library and Museum in London conserves the silver one that Roosevelt, then president of the United States of America, used to make his first Martini after the end of the Prohibition.

The shaker as it is well known is capable of cooling and mixing or emulsifying two or more products, even those that are difficult to mix.

Jerry Thomas used to embellish his shakers with precious stones, showcasing for the first time in history the art of pouring and making the preparation of the drink a truly entertaining moment for the customer.

The direct consequence of these discoveries associated with tonic allowed creating drinks that were less alcoholic, more diluted, cooler, and more thirst-quenching.

The 1900s was the century that greatly disrupted the customs and habits of the conviviality of good drinking.

Europe implemented a full-fledged crusade against alcoholism, as cases of cirrhosis and crimes became untenable.

Absinthe production, as well as that of some local spirits, was privatized. Drink lists were thus filled with fruit-based flavoring agents (maraschino cherry and orange peel infusions), and the resulting inventions were by far much sweeter and more feminine.

Americans followed in Europe's footsteps by declaring the state of Prohibition in the "Volstead Act": in force in the U.S. between 1919 and 1933, it established a ban on the manufacture, sale and importation of alcoholic products, also prohibiting their sale and consumption in bars. The Bureau of Prohibition was the federal agency created to enforce and apply this law.

A little bit of trivia: in Lynchburg, Tennessee, where the Jack Daniel's distillery has been located since 1866, some remnants of Prohibition still linger, since no establishment in the county is allowed to serve alcohol and only beer or wine can be purchased.

Prohibition represents the era of Al Capone and the Mafia, which terrorized the streets of metropolises. From 1920 onward, secret drinking establishments, the so-called "Speakeasies," sprang up.

Hidden clubs (mainly run by the underworld) that could only be accessed by knowing the password, also called "Blind Tiger," as some of them posed as attraction venues in which to admire stuffed tigers.

The Mafia also infiltrated alcohol production, resulting in smuggled products such as the famous "Moonshine," white whiskey made from the overnight distillation of rye and corn in illegal stills. Because of its strong and unpalatable taste, it was drunk diluted with water, sugar and lemon, the Whiskey Sour.

At the same time, the First World War broke out in Europe and whiskey disappeared.

Cocktail ingredients in that period are from the Allied States against Germany: gin, cognac, Cointreau and cherry brandy.

ITALY AND FUTURISM

Futurism was a very important Italian artistic and cultural movement in the history of innovation in the world of drinking and gastronomy.

In 1914, the French chef Jules Maincave joined Futurism, proposing the combination of new flavors or elements until then "separated without serious foundation." This included such juxtapositions as mutton fillet and shrimp sauce, veal sirloin and absinthe, banana and gruyere, and herring and strawberry jelly.

It was a period of great innovation and industrial growth, especially in the industrial triangle Milan-Turin-Genoa, which became the hub of the Futurist progress movement.

Cities "rose," lit up with electricity, and the fashion of drinking became increasingly linked to the concept of art: cocktails became true works of contemporary art.

Filippo Tommaso Marinetti, in an excerpt from "Futurist Cuisine," describes the period as one of the highest moments that international mixing has ever known.

The drinks, called "polibibites," which were deemed undrinkable and ditched by the Fascist period, not only had to taste good, but were to act as sexual stimulants and encourage the removal of inhibitory brakes in order to get explosive and provocative ideas.

The polibibites were divided into decisions (warm tonic polibibites for making important decisions), inventions (refreshing and mildly intoxicating polibibites for coming up with new ideas), in-bed-soon (winter warming poibibites), peace-in-bed (sleep-inducing polibibites), and war-in-bed (aphrodisiac and fertilizing polibibites).

They were not created by actual professional bartenders because no one with standard or classical training could limit the creative spirit in the drink in order to give the imagination free rein.

Dosage errors were welcome and allowed, so "every mistake will be able to give rise to a different recipe every time," said Marinetti. An example of a recipe published by Marinetti and Fillia in the book "Futurist Cuisine" was "The Great Waters" (polibibita by Futurist aeropainter Prampolini), which called for 1/4 grappa, 1/4 gin, 1/4 caraway, 1/4 anise and over the liquid a block of anchovy paste wrapped pharmaceutically in a wafer.

It changed the role of drinking (from smooth to very articulate), and the sweet-acidic pairing of punches was abandoned forever, to make way for "savory-sweet " or "sweet-spicy."

They were home-produced blends based on brandies, grappas, rosolio, absinthes but above all Italian vermouths: one stands out from them all, the famous "Giulio Cocchi," which played an active part in the Futurist period.

Spices became an active decoration and were used in the infusion of exotic fruits and flowers. They were the forerunners of homemade products that today every self-respecting bartender keeps on their bar: essences, bitters, and concentrates to be added in small doses to drinks.

Polibibites were meant to enhance conviviality and the bold dishes of Futurist cuisine, which was characterized by extreme care in preparing the "mise en place", as well as the abolition of cutlery, which was considered a stereotype of Italian cuisine and a limit to tactile sensation.

The sense of smell and taste were amplified by the combination of liquors, but also by music and noises, so that all the senses were engaged during the meal. The watchword of this dining experience was synesthesia: a perfect multisensory perception, in which aromas, flavors, and tactile interactions came together until they harmoniously merged into one extraordinary experience.

Sensory banquets were supposed to restore the richness of sensations by abandoning revelry and abundance, so much so that they declared war on pasta, which was thought to bring on drowsiness and slow digestion, exalting rice instead.

Etiquette called for sitting at the table without an appetite; the order of the courses was inverted and coffee could be served as an appetizer!

THE TIKI ERA

From the 1930s, the American middle class regained economic strength, to the point where they could afford to travel and spend vacations outside American borders, in search of a new way of life, aimed at escaping from the big cities that symbolized forced and obligatory progress; they sought an experience that approached a primitive essence, a life in contact with nature, an ancient and now lost spirituality.

Moreover, it was possible to indulge in the free consumption of alcoholic beverages without having the fear of being arrested.

Thanks to the foresight of some American tourists, the "exotic bar" took hold, recreating exotic establishments with an escapist atmosphere in and around Los

Angeles, embellished with lots of sand, palm trees and starfish.

The "Tiki Era" was born, becoming famous thanks to Ernest Raymond Beaumont-Gantt, who changed his name to Donn Beach, owner of the eponymous "Don the Beach-comber," a bar-restaurant with a Polynesian flair, which offered Cantonese cuisine and rum-based drinks, as well as brightly colored walls, furniture and décor based on floral motifs and plants of all kinds, a nod to South Seas culture.

His motto was: "If you can't get to paradise, I'll bring it to you". With exotic cocktails, Donn was able to evoke the atmospheres that people longed for and that he had actually experienced. Creating a preconceived cheerful environment brought people with considerable social differences together. Through Donn's infinite and clever engagement activities, they were united by the Punch at a "Luau," a Hawaiian party in which singing, dancing and traditions take place.

Donn Beach is unanimously considered the inventor of the Zombie, which was followed by two other legendary cocktails that are still popular today: the Scorpion Bowl and the Mai Tai first made by Victor Jules Bergeron Jr, founder of a chain of Polynesian-themed restaurants that bore his nickname, "Trader Vic".

After the end of Prohibition, the return to commercialization and the free market meant that rum began to flood the streets of America: a rum of excellent quality and countless organoleptic characteristics, so much so that one could boast of having up to forty or more different labels in one's establishment

For the first time in history, venues, increasingly attentive to the quality and variety of raw materials, offered unique cocktails and all-around sensory experiences to the public, which triggered a new fashion. It goes without saying that gin with increasingly original pairings also benefitted from this trend. We will see the Suffering Bastard, the most distinctive of the gin-based cocktails of the Tiki era, invented in 1942 and served inside a typically Hawaiian Moai-shaped glass called the Suffering Bastard Mug.

The flip side of the coin was the beginning of a period when consumption increased alarmingly, so much so that on June 10, 1935, the Association of Alcoholics Anonymous was founded in the United States, which later spread throughout the world. According to the history of this Association, that date corresponds to the day when Robert Smith, a physician and member of the Oxford Group, drank an alcoholic beverage for the last time, after thirty days of Bill Wilson working with him to promote abstinence from alcohol. The Oxford Group was the first organization, inspired by Evangelical Christians, made up of former alcoholics committed to fighting alcoholism, who later founded the Association of Alcoholics Anonymous.

During World War II, gin suffered another slump because war missiles used alcohol mixed with other flammable substances as their propellant, so the world's distilleries had to convert their grains into fuel.

Gin made from sugarcane, molasses and potatoes did not find favor with the public, so much so that it was considered a low value and poor product.

In 1949, George Orwell published the famous novel "1984" where, among other things, mention is made of "Victory Gin," a gin substitute of the lowest quality described as having "a sickly oily smell, similar to Chinese rice spirit."

In the 1950s, another distillate, vodka, which until then had been left on the fringes of the cocktail world, made its way into the limelight. A proponent of the popularization of vodka was the New York Times, which in a 1954 article discussed the vodka trend, recommending it with snacks adding lemon or orange zest to the bottle.

It is the era of the Screwdriver, a cocktail made of vodka and orange juice, belonging to the long drink category, which originated in a bar at the Park Hotel in New York City. There, Turkish secret agents seeking refuge from the Balkans and American engineers used to mix vodka with canned orange juice. Lacking a more suitable tool, they used a screwdriver to mix the ingredients, hence the name of the drink.

Instead, in Italy bitters such as Strega, Fernet and cordials, from Vov to Brancamenta and many others, became popular.

The spread of Anglo-Saxon culture promoted the habit of drinking, even in the Bel Paese, cocktails such as Martini and Gin and Tonic.

In fact, in 1948 Ernest Hemingway arrived in Venice, where he frequented the famous Hotel Gritti, the Florian and befriended Giuseppe Cipriani of Harry's Bar. In his novel entitled "Across the River and Into the Trees," he wrote: "The Colonel looked out of the windows and the door of the bar on to the waters of the Grand Canal. He could see the big black hitching post for the gondolas and the later afternoon winter light on the wind-swept water. Across the Canal was the old Palace and a wood barge, black and broad, was coming up the Canal, her bluff bows pushing up a wave even though she had the wind behind her. «Make it a very dry Martini» the Colonel said."

For Ernest Hemingway, the very dry martini was none other than the Montgomery, a cocktail inaugurated and named by the writer himself made with fifteen parts gin and one part vermouth. He had named it after the British general of the same name - whom he did not hold in high regard - who would not go into battle unless he outnumbered his opposition by 15 to 1.

Texts that talk about the revival of Made in Italy do not fail to mention gin, even though it is not among the leading products.

In the 1960s, on the other hand, gin was a well-known product, although in part considered poor, but it is clear that the aforementioned tradition of juniper rosolio has been completely forgotten. The skills and experience acquired by Italy - thanks to its extensive knowledge in the distillation and blending of herbs – was a fundamental impetus in the realization and marketing of new gins: the botanicals, that is, the herbs, spices, plants and roots that form the characteristic mix of a gin, define its flavor and aromas. They are countless and varied, even from country to country, that each taste of a new product reveals different and incomparable sensations and emotions.

Since the 1970s, gin has reentered drink lists with increasing prominence: Negroni, Gin and Tonic, Gin Lemon and Campari Gin.

In 1972, it was the turn of Negroni Sbagliato (or simply Sbagliato), a cocktail created at Bar Basso in Milan by bartender Mirko Stocchetto. It differs from the classic Negroni in that spumante brut replaces the gin. The drink is thus lighter due to the lower alcohol content.

From Spain, via the United Kingdom, all the way to France, the history of the Gin and Tonic reached its peak between 1980 and 1990. The spread of the cocktail first took place among students, then throughout the bars and cafes of Paris.

Instead, in Europe, the model of the discotheque meant as a meeting place and entertainment venue enjoys enormous success. Therefore, in the early 1980s, we see the construction of venues aimed at accommodating large crowds all over Europe, and in fact, the catchment area of discos is increasingly heterogeneous and less and less select. Dance clubs, which began in the early 1970s simply as ballroom venues, expanded during this period with new facilities adjacent to them to become "discotheques": in this way, managers increased and diversified their offerings of nighttime entertainment.

These were the years of the Long Island Iced Tea (a mix of equal parts of tequila, vodka, white rum, triple sec and gin with a splash of Coke) and Sex on the Beach created in 1987 during Spring Break in Fort Lauderdale.

In Italy, the 1980s and 1990s are certainly marked by the presence of a cocktail: the Angelo Azzurro. The original recipe is attributed to historic Roman bartender Giovanni "Mammina" and used gin, Cointreau and blue curaçao. It was never codified by the International Bartenders Association, which instead in 1987 regulated the Blue Lagoon in which gin is replaced by vodka.

The TGV, pronounced as in French for fast trains, is a real alcoholic bomb, very much in vogue in those years. TGV stands for tequila, gin and vodka. As for alcohol content, neither did the Invisible, which counts among its ingredients gin, rum, vodka and triple sec (sometimes the latter replaced by tequila).

THE CHALLENGE OF THE NEW MILLENNIUM

The success of gin is unquestionably celebrated with the new millennium: but what are the reasons behind all this success?

Actually, there are many and rather diverse reasons that can be traced back to both producers and consumers (the law of supply and demand).

Let's try to analyze the facts in order, well aware that in this new phase marketing is the undisputed protagonist, a determining factor in a product's diffusion.

First, drinking habits have changed. The moment of the aperitif has become increasingly central to everyone's life, and alongside the return of classic drinks such as the Spritz, Americano, and Negroni, the Gin and Tonic has also made its reappearance.

It appears from multiple sources that the reconquering of Europe by the Gin and Tonic originated in Spain this time, in the early 2000s, where they experimented with new ideas by turning a "club" drink into a refined and elegant cocktail, starting with serving it in the "Copa Balón," similar to wine glasses but more capacious and rounded. Perhaps it is precisely this resemblance to wine glasses, combined with the elegant presentation, which affirmed its increasing popularity as an aperitif.

The bitter component of the drink, in fact, naturally stimulates salivation, setting gastric juices in motion, which is ideal for a pre-dinner drink. In addition, the Gin and Tonic is versatile and easily paired, for example, with savory snacks, such as tacos, hamburgers, sushi and fried foods in general.

Another reason that should not be underestimated is its simple preparation, requiring "only" a good selection of gin and tonic waters at the base, but not the advanced technical or mnemonic skills of a bartender as with other drinks, such as Ramos Fizz or Singapore Sling just to name a few.

This simplicity of preparation has meant that venues such as day bars, coffee shops, restaurants, and pizzerias can offer it. An additional competitive advantage that venues have in offering this cocktail is the extreme shelf life of the ingredients. In fact, gin, if well stored, can last for many years, and tonic water has a shelf life of about three years, so the Gin and Tonic, unlike other cocktails that require fresh and perishable ingredients, such as juices or fruits, does not carry an "entrepreneurial risk."

The consumer on the other hand has perfectly understood the price range of a gin and tonic made with premium products, which even in non-specialized establishments and outside the big cities can be sold at above-average prices.

It is precisely consumers today who are more attentive to the quality of ingredients and therefore more likely to spend more to drink better.

The focus on calories has also increased considerably, and the Gin and Tonic is a low-calorie cocktail, even more so if a sugar-free tonic is used (50ml of 40 percent gin has about 100 calories).

On the production side, things get more complicated. The first factor to consider is definitely a general market trend: today people invest only after careful analysis, making a product based on market indications, in order to minimize business risk in all fields of consumption, from entertainment to automobiles.

Gin, unlike whiskey or rum, does not require aging and can be sold about sixty days after production, eliminating the entrepreneurial risk of capital tied up for years. The lion's share, however, is done by packaging and storytelling.

In fact, every bottle of gin placed on the market is the result of careful design studies, from the bottle to the label, and above all, every gin must tell the consumer a story, whether it is its historical heritage, its tie to a territory, or the use of a particular ingredient.

The first gin to bring about this revolution in the storytelling of the distillate seems to have been Hendrick's Gin, which placed itself in a higher price range while at the same time creating a narrative that is more easily understood by the entire public, not only as an image, but also as a service, by first proposing its "perfect cocktail serve", the now-iconic Gin and Tonic with cucumber slice.

Careful attention to packaging and product image are requisites for success. In fact, gin is chosen from the bottle rack of a club, where it is imperative to stand out among competing bottles. This is how you win in an industry that has been growing steadily for years, where new players enter the game every day and where the market is pulverized in sales by hundreds of Italian and foreign producers.

Although some fear an end to the modern "Gin Craze", the market shows no signs of waning, and in any case, all industry analysts agree that gin has changed the consumer's image of the spirit and it will never return to oblivion.

By now, quality and variety are fundamental for this product as well, just as for whiskies and rums, with the added benefit that very common gin-based cocktails number in the hundreds, therefore even in the future every bar must have at least a minimal selection of premium gins and tonics.

AND IN ITALY?

With the new millennium, Italian gin also becomes an established and developed product. To date there are numerous distilleries, with a very high concentration especially in Tuscany. There are over 400 "Made in Italy" labels, most of which are among the best on the world market and represent a concentrate of refinement and elegance. In the world, Italian gins are known above all for their characteristic of deviating from the classic London Dry Gin, proposing always new and sometimes bold combinations and scents, but with guaranteed impact.

Also contributing to the success of Italian gins is the number of first-rate plant varieties present in our territory and famous throughout the world. This is evident in a tendency to produce gins that could be defined as regional: we know how much each city or territory can be characterized by its own peculiarities, so we are beginning to see those links expressed with gin as well. We boast not only the largest production of juniper in the world, but also the greatest biodiversity, with thousands of potential indigenous ingredients with which to compose new gin recipes. In this regard, it will be increasingly common to hear customers ask, in addition to local wines, if the bars offer local gin.

CHAPTER II
Production

The base of gin is a distillate of a fermented base, usually cereal grains such as corn, wheat, and barley, and juniper berries, coriander seeds, and other aromatic herbs, basically a colorless product with alcohol content around forty percent.

The most common and widespread gins are English gins, made with a column still with a characteristic dry taste. Dutch gins, made with a "pot" still, are richer, more aromatic and fuller-bodied. Unlike the others, Dutch gins undergo an aging process of one to three years in oak barrels, which gives them a slight golden color. In Italy, a gin is made from the best juniper berries in the Mediterranean, and producers claim that its characteristics are similar to the drink produced by the friars of Alverna, in the Aretine region, in the 13th century.

There are several types of gin:

- the "classic" London dry gin, colorless, dry, fragrant, which may be referred to with the term "premium," indicating a higher alcohol content;

- Old Tom gin, colorless and made in England, sweetened with a small amount of sugar or sugar syrup, very popular in the 18th century. It probably got its name from the first vending machine that some English pubs had installed in the 1700s. Apparently, passers-by, after depositing a penny in the cat's mouth, would be served a shot of gin by the bartender through a small tube that reached outside to the customer's mouth. Sugar was added to try to mask the defects - the pungent, raw taste - due to the distillation method at the time;

- Plymouth gin, colorless, dry, with a very intense aroma and characteristic hints of roots, can only be produced in the Plymouth area of England, from which it takes its name. Plymouth gin boasts a storied history, as it was born in 1793 and is still produced today at the oldest working distillery. Plymouth gin, with its distinctive aroma, has been synonymous with cocktails since 1896, as it was used in the original Dry Martini. Plymouth gin has a rounded and aromatic smell and taste, where juniper is a predominant component, but with distinct and elegant notes of coriander, lemon and orange peel. It should be pointed out that this is a combination of Old Tom gin with London gin;

- Jenever gin, made in the Netherlands and aged in special earthenware vessels;

- Sloe gin, with a distinctive purple color, flavored with wild plums steeped in the product, then filtered and lightly sweetened;

- Pink gin, fortified with Angostura;

- Orange gin and Lemon gin, colorless and flavored with citrus essences.

PRODUCTION

There are many methods of producing gin, but European directives officially recognize only two: distilling and flavoring a spirit. Gin can be produced by three distinct techniques: distillation, percolation and maceration. Each of them allows the production of a drink with quite different characteristics and qualities.

The preparation of a liqueur may appear simpler than that of a distillate, despite the fact that the chemical industry makes extracts (concentrated substances and active ingredients) available to companies: many liqueur companies produce the essences necessary for production directly from plants.

In the preparation of gin, the sugar used is colorless and free of traces of iron, the water is organoleptically neutral and demineralized, and the juice of the fruits is squeezed and processed while still fresh. Distillation allows the separation, starting from a fermented must, of the alcoholic part by taking advantage of the boiling point of the various ingredients. There are two distillation techniques: the continuous method and the discontinuous method.

Distillation by the continuous method is carried out using stills that allow uninterrupted feeding of the raw material. With the discontinuous method, traditional stills are used, also placed in a row, where the distillate produced from one still is fed into another and distilled again. This process is useful in order to obtain a higher alcohol content and a purer product; in fact, from the first distillation, a product with an alcohol content of 28-30% is obtained; from the second distillation, it goes to much higher percentages (75-85%).

Distillation is not a linear procedure: it must be considered that a must is composed of different substances, including alcohols, esters and other volatile

substances, all of which have different boiling points and not all of which are suitable for making a good distillate. For this reason, in the distillation stage, there is a distinction between the production of three specific parts: the head, the heart, and the tail. During the first (head) and last (tail) stages, the less noble substances are carried away by the vapor current of ethyl alcohol and considered "polluting" and unpleasant, as well as dangerous to health, therefore they are eliminated. These three parts are not clearly distinguishable from each other: only an experienced master distiller, using appropriate instruments, can tell when the distillate coming out of the still possesses the characteristics that are considered suitable for commercialization.

The actual preparation of gin consists of a solution of water, alcohol, juniper berries and other aromatic substances placed in the still and left to rest at a temperature of 40-50° C for three days. At this point, distillation is carried out. The ethyl alcohol, during its evaporation, also drags the aromatic components of the herbs with it. Percolation is the process that takes advantage of a large container, similar to a large mocha pot, which is filled at the bottom with the hydroalcoholic solutions and in the center a basket of herbs and aromatic substances are left in suspension. The process begins by bringing the hydroalcoholic solution to a temperature of 50-60° C: as the vapors rise, they pass through the herbs, extracting the aromatic substances that settle to the bottom, mixing with the hydroalcoholic solution. This process lasts about two days, and at the end, the flavored hydroalcoholic solution is extracted from the container.

The maceration process is used when the aim is to extract as much aromatic essence as possible from the herbs or roots. The efficiency of the process depends on the fact that the aromatic substances are in direct contact with the solvent solution: the hydroalcoholic solution and all the aromatic herbs are placed in a container and kept at a temperature of 45-50° C for two weeks. Among the gin production systems, the most relevant is distillation, used to produce London dry gin and Plymouth gin. The other, less widely used method is that of aromatizing a spirit, technically known as compounding: gins produced by this method have a predominant aroma of juniper. In this method, the alcohol takes on crucial importance: it must be a particularly neutral spirit and possibly have an alcohol content of at least 96%.

TASTING IN PURITY

For the proper tasting of a distillate, first of all, an isolated, low-noise environment that is not influenced by extraneous scents is required; then it is necessary to choose the right glass, preferably tulip-shaped, clean and odorless; finally, water with a low salt content. If the tasting involves several spirits, it is important to start with the most delicate one.

Pour the distillate into the glass and sniff (caution: inhaling for too long has an "anesthetizing" effect on the olfactory papillae, as our sensorial organs tend to ignore an odor that permeates them for too long).

Close the glass with the palm of your hand and with your other hand take the glass between your middle and ring fingers, swirl it gently enough to agitate the distillate, open the top of the glass and sniff again. This serves to perceive with greater depth even the most delicate and evanescent aromas.

Then dilute the distillate with water in order to allow the other aromas to be released and rise toward the opening of the glass. Add the same amount of water as the distillate in the glass. Continue until the last olfactory sensations are perceived.

Sip some of the distillate by letting it run over your tongue as to capture every nuance of the key flavors; the previously diluted distillate will be well tolerated by the taste buds. Swallow, analyzing the various nuances and their persistence in the mouth, that is, the amount of time the taste sensations continue to be perceived.

Initially it will not be easy to distinguish scents and flavors, but with proper training and enough practice, it will be possible to recognize, isolate, and distinguish the various sensory perceptions.

CHAPTER III
Gin & Tonic, the cocktail

The word cocktail immediately conjures up relaxation, chatting, and the freedom that accompanies an appetizer in the company of others. Having an aperitif has now become a pleasurable ritual, a true liturgy, which is popular in clubs and, increasingly, at home.

The perfect cocktail must have a balanced structure, aroma and color. Various alcoholic, non-alcoholic and flavoring ingredients can be present in the mix.

The Gin and Tonic is a long drink made from gin and tonic water, now among the most famous and iconic.

Personally, I approached this cocktail because of the absence of dyes and other undesirable substances, which I find superfluous in good drinks, which means that when ordering or buying tonic water it is necessary to read the label carefully. Even without being an expert on the subject, a very long list of ingredients is synonymous with a highly industrialized product, and this is a rule I follow for all food as well (the fewer ingredients a product has, the more genuine and natural it is).

The essential components of a good tonic are water, cane sugar, citric acid, natural quinine, and natural flavors. The rest is superfluous.

There are numerous variations of this drink depending on the context: whether as an aperitif (pre-dinner) or after dinner. In addition, thanks to the remarkable varieties of gin and tonic that have developed in recent years, excellent food pairings are possible and therefore you can continue drinking it throughout the meal. If you ever happen to be in Hong Kong or Singapore, I highly recommend trying out some good lounge bars where you can find cocktails paired with sushi - a universe of flavors and experiences to try!

With a few tips on how to make artful drinks and the best cocktail sets, it will be easy and fun to impress your guests. The first thing that should not be lacking is imagination, especially for presentation, as well as fresh ingredients and selected liqueurs or soft drinks (remember that every gin has its own tonic). Next, the right tools are needed, considering a complete set will be much less expensive than buying the individual pieces separately. It is imperative to choose products made of food-grade steel, the best being AISI 316 stainless steel; this steel is particularly suitable for contact with food, as it has high resistance to acids, bases and chlorides, such as salt. Other austenitic stainless steels, such as 304, can develop pitting (sur-

face corrosion). 316 is immune to this type of corrosion and therefore suitable for almost all applications.

Shaker: it is the tool you use to mix ingredients. Some models have a built-in strainer, while others have a graduated cap that is useful for measuring doses. The shaker should be held horizontally and shaken vigorously with both hands for about 15 seconds, the time needed for the metal to frost. As a rule, carbonated beverages should never be placed inside, as they will deflate and cause the shaker to open. If you do not have a shaker, you can alternatively use a large jar, with a cap similar to those used for preserves, which has a capacity of at least 500 ml.

Strainer: it is placed on top of the shaker, so the diameter must match. It allows the drink to be strained from any ice fragments or fruit residue.

Bar spoon or stirrer: it is a particular long and spiral-shaped spoon, which is used to mix long drinks or cocktails that are not shaken.

Measuring cup or jigger: a graduated glass, useful for measuring the amounts of different ingredients. As a rule, the amount of alcohol should not exceed 5 to 7 centiliters.

THE RECIPE AND HOW TO MAKE IT

The first step is to fill the glass (a tall tumbler or balloon) with large ice cubes until it is filled to the brim and beyond. Using little ice runs the risk that it will melt, diluting the cocktail and making it watered down. In addition, a nice glass filled with clinking ice has a dramatic effect, while a glass with few ice cubes will drastically quash the drink's aesthetic and gustatory performance.

Many people explicitly request little ice, but the result is that the drink will be more diluted, because the little ice added will melt more rapidly and, even worse, the cocktail will not be at the right serving temperature.

Therefore, at home preparing for a gathering with friends, I always recommend buying a few bags of ready-made ice, strictly with at least 30-gram full cubes. Smaller-sized ice cubes melt faster, as does ice prepared at home in molds or bags. If you really want to prepare it yourself, I suggest taking a plastic food container, filling it with filtered, boiled water and letting it freeze. After that, break the ice mass with a serrated knife in order to split shards to add to your cocktail, guaranteeing special effects and the cocktail will be served at the correct temperature.

Before using the ice, it is a good idea to leave it out of the freezer for a few minutes so it moistens on the surface: this will help the tonic from going flat.

Always chill the glass before each use: the warm surface of the glass will prematurely melt the ice.

Having filled the glass with ice, pour in 40 to 60 ml of gin; my advice is to stick to 40 ml for an aperitif cocktail, while you are allowed to go up to 60 ml for an after dinner drink.

Do not make the mistake of pouring the entire contents of the tonic bottle into the glass: the tonic should usually be added in proportion to the amount of gin (two parts tonic to one part gin). In other words, a typical Gin and Tonic with 50 ml of gin will require about 100 ml of tonic.

Another mistake one can run into is using tonic water at room temperature: this will inevitably melt the ice, watering down the cocktail. Therefore, use tonic water at refrigerator temperature.

When the tonic is added, the gin and tonic should be lightly stirred with a bar spoon, the long-handled spoon perfect for deeply mixing the cocktail from the bottom up. It is necessary especially if a tall tumbler has been chosen as the glass.

Stirring the drink gently, to avoid it going flat, I recommend adding a few more ice cubes with tongs so that it literally flows out of the glass.

Finish preparing the gin and tonic with a garnish based on the type of gin used: you can look for a pairing flavor or one that enhances an ingredient already in the gin. Therefore, not only the classic slice of lemon, rather you can experiment with variants such as lime, cucumber, grapefruit (perfect for aromatic gins because they add a fresh note), apple (with herbaceous gins), fresh ginger, orange peel (with spiced gins), star anise, cocoa bean, a sprig of lavender, basil or rosemary. If you opt for a peel, it should be edible therefore use organic fruit.

What I do not find elegant are spices added to the surface, which make sipping the drink difficult. Therefore, no floating juniper berries or pepper corns, which, if chewed could anesthetize the taste buds, impeding you from fully tasting the drink. Moreover, they contribute to making the gin and tonic go flat sooner.

The carbon dioxide contained in the tonic is in tiny bubbles held together by strong bonds. This solution is not stable and when you shake a bottle, the bubbles join and become bigger, resulting in a fizzing jet. Therefore, the tonic water must be poured gently. There is also the phenomenon of nucleation, which occurs when the bubbles meet a rough surface (for example, ice just taken out of the freezer and therefore not damp) or granules (ground pepper, etc.).

WHICH GLASS SHOULD I USE?

In order to make an impeccable gin and tonic, the choice of an adequate glass must not be overlooked. Each cocktail – as each alcoholic beverage – has a specific type of glass, which on one hand enhances its properties and on the other is the fruit of stylistic and customary choices. Choosing the wrong glass is a bit like putting an ugly frame on a work of art: you risk not enhancing the content and in some cases ruining it.

With regard to making the best gin and tonic, two glasses are indicated, the tumbler and the balloon glass. The tumbler is tall and the most used for serving long drinks in general. However, we now see it increasingly served in a balloon glass, very common in Spain (where it is called copa de balón), which, thanks to the stem, the ice does not melt so fast. The latter is my favorite glass, above all if served at the table with a meal.

TONIC WATER: THE OBSCURE INGREDIENT

As previously mentioned, tonic water must be added in the ratio of one part gin, two parts tonic, even though many bartenders serve it at 1:3 or even reaching 1:4. The thing to point out, however, is that regardless of the direction of thinking, tonic water represents the main ingredient by quantity; yet this aspect is often completely underestimated. The same amount of time spent on the search for a good gin should also be spent on the evaluation of a good tonic to go with it: not all tonics fit all gins. The perfect gin and tonic recipe is strictly personal and subjective. That is why the bartender should ask about preferred notes in order to recommend the ideal pairing.

On the positive side, the explosion in the number of gins available on the market has been followed by an interesting variety of premium tonics, placing greater emphasis on the use of natural quinine over artificial flavoring. Perhaps the only real rule of thumb is just that: read the ingredients well to understand whether the product is premium or not.

There are four main types of tonic water: classic, botanical, flavored, and light.

Classic tonic waters, also called "Indian," have a clean, dry, bitter taste, often enhanced by a citrus note (such as lime, grapefruit, lemon or orange) to balance the note imparted by quinine and the dry note imparted by gin.

"Indian" tonics are considered pure in that they normally contain only the essential ingredients: water, carbon dioxide, sugar, and natural quinine bark extract.

Botanical tonics are flavored with herbs or with edible flowers such as rosemary, thyme, and myrtle or linden blossoms, which lend a refined note to the traditional tonic taste.

Flavored tonics are olfactively pervasive and often have a characterizing note. These tonic waters are definitely the most difficult to pair, mainly because they risk overpowering the taste of the gin and, in my opinion, are at their best when drunk neat.

Light tonics have fewer calories and sugar is replaced with artificial sweeteners (saccharin) or natural sweeteners (stevia), which an attentive palate will certainly notice. Is the result better or worse? Again, the answer is entirely subjective.

THE 10 COMMANDMENTS FOR A GOOD GIN & TONIC

The following is a recap of the rules for making an excellent Gin & Tonic before moving on to the actual preparation:

1. Thoroughly chill the glass;
2. Use large and full ice cubes;
3. Do not use ice that has just come out of the freezer, rather leave it at room temperature a few minutes before using it;
4. Before adding the ingredients to the glass, drain any water from diluted ice;
5. Pour from 40 to 60 ml of gin into the glass;
6. Use cold tonic water, never at room temperature, bout 100 ml (I recommend the ratio of 1:2 with gin);

7. Do not engage in useless "acrobatics" or superfluous virtuosity, such as pouring the tonic along the bar spoon, you will only make the tonic flat;
8. Add more ice so that it comes out of the drink;
9. Garnish as desired;
10. The success of the drink is not due to spices or other added elements. On the contrary, you will risk making it go flat more quickly. Instead, you can use a twist of citrus zest, letting the essential oils come out through a twist or other spices, but always on the outside of the glass.

CHAPTER IV
Other ways to say Gin & Tonic

In the following, I propose some recipes that, without horrifying purists, can be alternatives to the classic Gin & Tonic. Not just a variation, but more complex recipes that add other flavors and complexity to the well-known drink or tone down its bitter note. In this sense, these recipes can be an approximation to the actual Gin & Tonic, serving as a link between markedly sweet and mellow drinks to cocktails with stronger and more assertive flavors.

Gin Tonic ~ Grapefruit

- 45 ml of gin
- 30 ml of fresh grapefruit juice
- 15 ml of sugar syrup
- 15 ml of fresh lime juice
- 60 ml of tonic water

How to make

Fill a tall tumbler or balloon glass with ice and add all the ingredients. Gently stir.

Garnish with a grapefruit slice.

To make sugar syrup, pour equal parts of caster sugar and water into a pan on low heat. Stir with a clean stainless-steel spoon until the sugar has dissolved then let cool.

Gin Tonic ~ Peach and thyme

- 50 ml of gin
- 100 ml of tonic water
- 5 slices of fresh peach
- Thyme sprig

How to make

Wet a tall tumbler and put it in the freezer for 5 minutes. Using a kitchen torch, burn a sprig of thyme, immediately covering it with the glass to make sure to trap the fumes given off.

Now fill the glass with ice and add the gin and tonic water. Using tongs, insert peach slices at various levels into the glass. For the best result, it is important to use a tasty, ripe but firm peach to prevent it from falling apart. An excellent alternative to peach is mango.

Gin Tonic ~ Spring summer

- 45 ml of gin
- 100 ml of tonic water
- 15 ml of St. Germain
- 15 ml of fresh lime juice
- 1 cucumber
- 4 basil leaves

How to make

Pour the gin, St. Germain, lime juice, ice and basil leaves into a shaker and shake until the metal is frosty. Double strain and pour into a tall tumbler full of ice. Add the tonic water and using tongs, put cucumber strips into the drink (the strips can be made using a mandolin slicer or a potato peeler).

Finish with some ice cubes until the drink literally overflows and garnish with basil and a slice of lime.

Gin Tonic ~ Hawaii

- 50 ml of gin
- 70 ml of pineapple juice (without added sugar)
- 15 ml of fresh lime juice
- Tonic water to top off
- Fresh or canned pineapple

How to make

Grill two slices of fresh or canned pineapple until the surface is caramelized on both sides. One slice will be used as a garnish, while the other must be cut into pieces and put in a shaker with the ice, gin, pineapple juice and lime. Shake well and strain into a balloon glass filled with ice and top with tonic water. Alternatively, use Prosecco instead of tonic water.

Gin Tonic ~ Pink rose

- 45 ml of gin
- 1 teaspoon rose water
- 15 ml of fresh lime juice
- 15 ml of sugar syrup
- 100 ml of tonic water

How to make

Pour all the ingredients into a high tumbler full of ice and stir with a bar spoon until mixed.

Garnish with edible rose petals (many shops now sell containers of edible flowers) and a slice of lime.

Gin Tonic ~ Cherry

- 45 ml of gin
- 5 fresh cherries
- 15 ml of fresh lime juice
- 100 ml of tonic water

How to make

Stone the cherries and press them lightly, taking care to recover any juice released. Place in tall tumbler filled with ice along with the gin and lime juice. Give it an initial stir and then add the tonic and then gently stir the drink to prevent it from going flat. The result will be a delicate and tasty gin and tonic with an inviting red color.

The same drink can be prepared by replacing the cherries with another fresh fruit, such as raspberries, blueberries or blackberries.

The method will be the same after obtaining a puree by pounding the chosen fruit. The important thing is to use seasonal fruit, which will definitely turn out tastier.

As an additional variation, it is possible to add a few drops of raspberry vinegar, a special ingredient that will enhance the taste of the cocktail.

Gin Tonic ~ Mediterranean

- 50 ml of gin
- 100 ml of tonic water
- 30 ml of sugar syrup
- Sprig of thyme and/or rosemary
- 2 sage leaves
- 15 ml of fresh lemon juice
- 15 ml of fresh orange juice

How to make

First, prepare the sugar syrup by heating equal parts of water and sugar with the addition of the thyme, rosemary and sage.

In case it turns out too thick, add a little more water.

Once the scented syrup has cooled, pour the right amount into a tall tumbler filled with ice along with all the other ingredients and mix well with a bar spoon.

Add a few ice cubes and garnish with lemon and orange zest. Avoid adding herbs to the garnish, so as not to over-mark the herbaceous hints already present in the drink.

Gin Tonic ~ Orange and cinnamon

- 60 ml of Old Tom Gin
- 120 ml of tonic water
- Orange
- 1 cinnamon stick

How to make

Quickly flame the cinnamon stick and insert it in a tall balloon glass with plenty of ice along with the gin and tonic.

Twist the orange peel on the glass to release the essential oils and put a thin slice of orange between the ice and the glass.

Do not use cinnamon powder - it will cover the other flavors and get in the way when sipping the drink.

Gin Tonic ~ Strawberries and balsamic vinegar

- 60 ml of London Dry Gin
- 100 ml of tonic water
- 1 ripe strawberry
- Fresh ginger
- 15 ml of aged balsamic vinegar
- 15 ml of lemon juice
- 15 ml of sugar syrup

How to make

Pour the gin, lemon juice and sugar syrup, and finally the tonic water into a tall tumbler filled with ice. Stir from the bottom to the top.

Cut the fresh ginger and strawberry lengthwise into thin strips and lay them between the glass and the ice.

Just before serving or even better in front of guests slowly pour the balsamic vinegar (vinegar aged 12 years is recommended), trying to form spots within the cocktail. If you do not have aged balsamic vinegar, you can use vinegar glaze but reduce the amount of sugar syrup. Regular balsamic vinegar is too acidic and will also uniformly color the drink.

Gin Tonic ~ Spicy Tomato

- 60 ml of gin
- 60 ml of tonic water
- 60 ml of tomato juice
- Worcestershire sauce
- Fine salt
- 15 ml of fresh lime juice
- Tabasco

How to make

In an ice-filled shaker, place all the ingredients except the tonic water. Worcestershire sauce and tabasco should be dosed according to your taste; try a couple of dashes of both at first. Shake until the metal is frosted. Strain and pour into a tumbler previously filled with ice and add the tonic a little at a time. Finally stir gently and add a few more ice cubes.

Garnish with a red bullhorn pepper, a few thin slices of cucumber and lime.

Try adding a little powdered meat flavoring agent to the shaker, making sure to pound it well with a mortar to make a very fine, firm mixture.

To make the tomato juice, take ripe tomatoes and blend them until smooth and homogeneous. Strain well through a fine-mesh strainer and then refrigerate at least a couple of hours before using.

Always favor homemade juice and preparations: those on the market often have food additives and added sugars.

CHAPTER V
Recipe book

The following, as well as the previously illustrated explanation on how to make a gin and tonic, are recipes that are the fruit of years of study, experimentation and trial and error, not always spot on, in order to give my guests an experience to remember. To do this, one not only has to mix the ingredients well, but first has to procure top-quality raw materials and then think about everything else. Yes, because a true experience involves all the senses: visually striking garnishes and the right glass are essential to impact sight, added aromas and essential oils or smoking will soothe the sense of smell, a particular glass to handle will give new tactile sensations, and good music will please the ear. These are the indispensable elements that make up the perfect drink!

The amounts given, where possible, are based exactly on those published and established by the IBA (International Bartenders Association), but they are not "law"- experience, personal taste, and creative flair can lead to modifying quantities in order to achieve your perfect drink.

Where the exact name of a bottle is indicated, it is because that is how the recipe intended it. On the other hand, with regard to the item "juice of..." it is always recommended to squeeze fresh fruit at the time. Usually, store-bought juices contain added sugars and/or other unwanted ingredients. The same goes for syrups.

I will never tire of repeating that the success or failure of a drink is determined nine times out of ten by the ice: choose either to buy it (full cubes of about thirty grams) or to prepare it by following the aforementioned procedure to the letter.

Begin each recipe by pouring plenty of ice into the serving glass to chill it (lesser quality ice can also be used in this case), then devote yourself to reading and then the actual preparation. Before pouring the liquid into the glass remember to empty the glass and add new ice if the recipe calls for it.

If you want to amaze your friends with easy, yet impressive decorations, I recommend buying a dryer you can use to create delicious, healthy and natural snacks such as apple chips, banana chips, mango chips, etc. For example, a nice slice of dried orange is perfect for garnishing a Negroni.

The last secret to a good cocktail is being able to combine the right flavor with the right person, and you will see that every time they are your guest, they will ask you, "Would you make me the same drink as last time?" Try it to believe it!

Negroni

- 30 ml of gin
- 30 ml of Campari
- 30 ml of sweet red vermouth

How to make

Negroni is one of the most famous Italian cocktails in the world: it has an unmistakable taste and is served in a low tumbler filled with ice. A must is a scented slice of orange, which you should remove the seeds from and slice thinly, so that it will lie between the ice cubes and slightly stick out from the drink.

Before serving give it a gentle stir and perfume the surface of the glass with an orange twist: make a thin peel and gently twist to release the essential oils contained in it.

Gimlet

- 60 ml of Plymouth Gin
- 15 ml of lime juice
- 5 ml of sugar syrup

How to make

Place all ingredients in a shaker and shake with ice until the metal surface is frosted.

Pour into a champagne glass and add a single large ice cube and garnish with a slice of lime. Do not use seltzer.

The first mention of this cocktail dates back to 1928 when gin was dosed almost pure with only a few drops of lime juice. Later the recipe was revived by mixing equal parts gin and lime juice. So try varying the proportions among the three ingredients to achieve the balance that suits you.

Pegu Club

- 60 ml of gin
- 30 ml of Curaçao
- 15 ml of lime juice
- 1 dash of Angostura

How to make

Place all ingredients in a shaker and shake with ice until the metal surface is frosted.

Pour into a previously chilled cocktail glass and garnish with a lime twist or grapefruit slice.

The Pegu is a cocktail invented around 1927 at the Pegu Club. The club was located just outside Yangon, also known at one time as Rangoon, the largest city in Myanmar (formerly Burma), and its patrons were mostly high-ranking British officials, military personnel, and businessmen. The club was named after the river of the same name.

White Lady

- 40 ml of gin
- 30 ml of Triple Sec
- 20 ml of lemon juice

How to make

First, fill a cocktail glass with ice and allow the glass to cool. After that pour all the ingredients into a shaker along with a generous amount of ice and shake vigorously until frosted on the surface.

At this point, empty the cup and pour in the contents of the shaker, using a strainer.

Serve immediately without a straw.

London Mule

- 45 ml of gin
- 120 ml of ginger beer
- 10 ml of lime juice

How to make

This is the English variant of the Moscow Mule, a drink officially recognized by the IBA, which involves substituting vodka with gin.

Pour the ingredients into a highball glass and garnish with a lime wedge.

Sometimes you will find it served in a copper glass; be careful, however, to check that the copper is not in direct contact with the drink, as it may be poisonous. Copper glasses are coated on the inside with other materials or metals precisely to prevent the acidity of the liquid from reacting and releasing harmful substances.

Gin Fizz

- 45 ml of gin
- 30 ml of lemon juice
- 10 ml of sugar syrup*
- A splash of soda water

How to make

First start by chilling a tall tumbler by filling it with ice. This step is very important, because eventually this drink will have to be served without ice, so it is necessary to avoid warming the liquid in any way.

Place all the ingredients inside an ice-filled shaker and shake vigorously. When the shaker is frosted, strain into the glass after emptying the ice.

Finally, add a splash of soda to spice up the drink. There have been "disposable" soda siphons on the market for a few cents for a long time now, which are very convenient for home use.

* Sugar syrup can be purchased in a bottle, but you can make it at home quickly and easily by putting equal parts of water and caster sugar in a small saucepan and bringing it to a boil, stirring until all the sugar is dissolved, then remove from the heat and let it cool before storing in the refrigerator. Properly stored in the refrigerator it can last for about a month.

Monkey Gland

- 45 ml of Dry Gin
- 45 ml of fresh orange juice
- 1 teaspoon of absynthe
- 1 teaspoon of Grenadine syrup

How to make

A very tasty cocktail that is easy to make. Start by chilling a cocktail glass by filling it with ice. Pour all the ingredients into a shaker with ice and shake well until the shaker is frosted. Pour the liquid into the glass after draining it.

Garnish with orange zest or perhaps a slice of dried orange.

Bramble

- 50 ml of gin
- 25 ml of fresh lemon juice
- 12.5 ml of sugar syrup
- 15 ml of Crème de Mûre

How to make

Crème de Mûre is a blackberry liqueur. I personally use the one by Maison Edmond Briottet with an alcohol content of 18%. It is very good to drink pure, as an after-dinner drink served chilled (about 14° C).

To prepare the cocktail, put all the ingredients, except the Crème de Mûre, in a shaker and with ice until the metal surface is frosted.

Pour into an old fashioned glass previously filled with broken ice*. At this point also pour in the Crème de Mûre in a circular motion.

Garnish to taste with a slice of lemon and fresh blackberries to reinforce the cocktail flavor.

*Broken ice is not crushed ice. Broken ice is defined as full ice cubes, possibly purchased, placed in a cloth bag or inside a clean kitchen towel and broken into not-too-small pieces with a meat tenderizer or any other heavy object. Never use pieces of ice or crushed ice that are too small in order to avoid watering down the drink.

Singapore Sling

- 30 ml of gin
- 15 ml of Cherry liqueur
- 7.5 ml of Cointreau
- 7.5 ml of DOM Bénédictine
- 120 ml of fresh pineapple juice
- 15 ml of fresh lime juice
- 10 ml of Grenadine syrup
- 1 dash of Angostura

How to make

Begin by chilling the glass, i.e. filling a 420-280-ml hurricane glass with ice. Then pour all the ingredients into a shaker previously filled with plenty of ice and shake vigorously until frosted on the surface. Drain the water from the melted ice from the glass and pour the liquid, always using a strainer.

Garnish with a pineapple slice and a Maraschino cherry.

It is advisable to respect the doses and ingredients given to the letter. In particular, the juice should be lime and not lemon; although they are similar-looking fruits, the taste differs: lemon is tarter, while lime is more sour.

Finally, if you are wondering what to use in place of DOM Bénédictine (a very special and old herbal liqueur), I suggest you change cocktails. Any other substitute would not give you the Singapore Sling.

Please note: the alcohol content and therefore the alcoholic perception in your mouth with this cocktail is about 10% (less than a glass of wine), which might lead you to drink more than one, but the amount of alcohol in it is 17.2 grams. Just to give an example, gin and tonic has an average alcohol content of 14%, but it contains 15 grams of alcohol. In other words, gin and tonic is stronger in the mouth, but with less alcohol ingested.

CHERRY

Smoked Gin

- 50 ml of gin
- 10 ml of tonic
- Maple wood chips
- Rosemary
- Pepper corns
- Citrus zest

How to make

Rinse a tall tumbler glass with water and then place it in the freezer for about 15 minutes or at least until the light film of water has frozen. This step is critical because it will retain the smokiness.

Using a kitchen torch, flame the chips, peppercorns, rosemary and some citrus peels to taste on a hard, non-flammable surface.

Cover with the chilled tumbler and wait a few moments for the smoke generated to go all the way to the surface of the tumbler.

After that, as with a regular gin and tonic, fill the glass to the brim with ice, add the gin and finally the tonic, using a stirrer to prevent it from going flat. Finally, a gentle stir from the bottom up and the drink is ready.

There are different types of smokers on the market. Personally, I prefer a regular blowpipe, which is cheaper but also more durable and longer lasting. Wood chips are usually sold online or in stores that specialize in barbecue.

Try changing wood essences and perhaps adding other spices, for example, a particular and sought-after pairing is olive wood and thyme.

John Collins

- 45 ml of Old Tom Gin*
- 30 ml of fresh lemon juice
- 15 ml of sugar syrup
- 60 ml of soda

How to make

Place all ingredients directly into a cylindrical-shaped highball glass (tumbler type with a capacity between 240 and 350 ml) and using a stirrer, stir gently in a circular motion from bottom to top.

Garnish with a lemon slice and a Maraschino cherry.

*Old Tom Gin is a type of gin that that differs in the addition of sugar, resulting in a product that tends to be sweeter and softer to the palate.

Bee's Knees

- 52.5 ml of Dry Gin
- 2 teaspoons of honey
- 22.5 ml of fresh lemon juice
- 22.5 ml of fresh orange juice

How to make

Dissolve the honey along with the lemon and orange juices, and then add the gin. Pour into a shaker with ice cubes. Shake vigorously, strain and pour into a cocktail glass previously chilled with ice and then drained.

As a garnish, add lemon or orange zest to taste.

This cocktail dates back to the Prohibition period, when it was necessary to use various sweeteners to improve the flavor of spirits, but the result was a fantastic and timeless cocktail.

Clover Club

- 45 ml of gin
- 15 ml of raspberry syrup
- 15 ml of fresh lemon juice
- 10 ml of egg white

How to make

An elegant drink with a unique acidity and sweetness. To make it, you need to place all the ingredients in a shaker with ice and shake vigorously for at least thirty seconds: this is first and foremost to incorporate air as well as to chill.

Then pour the mixture into a cocktail glass previously chilled with ice and then emptied.

Garnish with fresh raspberries skewered with a toothpick.

Raspberry syrup is very simple to make at home: start with fresh raspberries, of course, which must be crushed and sieved to remove the seeds. Then put the mixture in a pot with lemon and sugar: for a tub of raspberries weighing an average of 125 grams, add 200 grams of sugar and the juice of one lemon. Once it reaches a boil, turn it off and let it cool well before using.

The syrup can be stored in the refrigerator for a few days.

Ramos Fizz

- 45 ml of gin
- 15 ml of fresh lemon juice
- 15 ml of fresh lime juice
- 30 ml of sugar syrup
- 60 ml of cream
- 30 ml of egg white
- 3 dashes of orange blossom water
- 2 dashes of vanilla extract*
- Soda

How to make

Add all ingredients (except soda) to a shaker with ice for at least two minutes.

Then pour the cocktail into a highball glass, without the ice, using the strainer and a fine-mesh strainer. Top with a soda, which will cause the drink to develop the typical froth on the surface.

*Do not use vanillin in place of vanilla extract; the taste would be irreparably affected. Vanillin is a synthetic flavoring, that is, a molecule that is chemically obtained with a markedly unnatural taste.

A bit of trivia to tell your guests: the cocktail was invented in 1888 by Henry C. Ramos while working at his bar in New Orleans, Louisiana, the Imperial Cabinet Saloon.

The cocktail was originally called the "New Orleans Fizz," and to make it, some 30 bartenders were hired at the bar in charge of the exclusive preparation of this drink: they would shake for more than 12 minutes passing the shaker one after the other before pouring and serving. Imagine the choreography!

French 75

- 30 ml of gin
- 15 ml of fresh lemon juice
- 15 ml of sugar syrup
- 60 ml of champagne

How to make

You could say that the French 75 is a French-style John Collins, a sophisticated, easy and quick version to make for an aperitif, perhaps accompanied by raw scampi or smoked salmon.

To begin, place all ingredients - except the champagne - in a shaker with ice and shake until the surface is frosted. Pour the strained liquid into a previously chilled flute. Finally, add the champagne gently and stir.

Garnish with a lemon peel.

Dry Martini

- 60 ml of gin
- 10 ml of dry vermouth

How to make

This well-known drink is nothing more than gin "dirtied" with white vermouth and chilled. The technique used is called "Stir & Strain": the cocktail is stirred in the mixing glass with ice and then strained into the previously chilled glass. In this case, it is advisable to leave the glass in the freezer for about ten minutes.

Finish the drink with a twist of lemon to release the essential oils on the surface and accompany with the must-have olive served on the side.

A bit of trivia: Queen Elizabeth II inherited a passion for "Gin and Dubonnet" from her mother. This cocktail consists of three parts Dubonnet and seven of gin, a squeeze of lime and lots of ice. The monarch usually drank a glass before meals.

Last Word

- 22.5 ml of gin
- 22.5 ml of Green Chartreuse*
- 22.5 ml of Maraschino Luxardo
- 22.5 ml of fresh lemon juice

How to make

Place all ingredients in a chilled shaker and shake vigorously until the metal is frosted. Pour by straining the contents into a previously chilled small cocktail glass (maximum capacity 10 cl).

Important: Do not add garnishes. The color of the drink (pale green) with its complex, rich hints will speak for itself.

The Last Word is a strong cocktail (with an alcohol content of about 30 percent), as well as edgy, aromatic, easy to make, but impossible to forget. Definitely worth trying. Invented and consumed in 1920, at the height of the Prohibition period, it was rediscovered in the early years of the new millennium and only in 2020 did it fully enter the list of cocktails officially recognized by the IBA (International Bartenders Association).

*Green Chartreuse is a liqueur with an alcohol content of 55 percent, produced according to a secret recipe by distilling a maceration of as many as 130 different herbs and medicinal plants. It takes on a natural yellow-green color and is left to mature in oak barrels. Try neat over ice at the end of a meal.

Bijou

- 40 ml of gin
- 30 ml of sweet vermouth
- 15 ml di Green Chartreuse
- 1 dash of Orange Bitter

How to make

It is very simply prepared in the mixing glass with ice, stirring gently to mix the ingredients well. Then pour it into a goblet or even better into an old-fashioned glass, preferably with a large chunk of ice.

This is a recipe dating back to the 1890s, created by Harry Johnson, who with Jerry Thomas and William Schmidt, was the founding father of the socalled modern American bartending.

The name appears to come from the colors of three jewels: gin for diamond, vermouth for ruby, and Chartreuse for emerald.

The Bijou has been popular for several decades. Unlike the Manhattan and Martini, however, Bijou disappeared after the Prohibition. It was rediscovered by "the king of cocktails," Dale DeGroff, in the 1980s when he came across the recipe in Johnson's book. While the original cocktail had equal parts of the three ingredients, DeGroff tripled the ratio of gin, vermouth and Chartreuse to soften the flavor profile. Eventually, his recipe became the standard.

Vesper

- 45 ml of gin
- 15 ml of vodka
- 7.5 ml of Lillet Blanc

How to make

Place all ingredients in a shaker filled with ice and shake until the metal is frosted. "Shaken, not stirred," James Bond's famous phrase in the film "Casino Royal," the origin of the recipe dictated by the star to the waiter and then christened "Vesper" in honor of his beloved.

Pour by straining the contents into a previously chilled cocktail glass (Martini glass).

Garnish with a long thin slice of lemon peel.

Lillet Blanc is a wine-based liqueur born in 1872 in Pondesac, south of Bordeaux. It is a secret blend of 85% wine and fruit infusions.

Aviation

- 45 ml of gin
- 15 ml of Maraschino Luxardo
- 15 ml of fresh lemon juice
- 1 teaspoon of Crème de Violette*

How to make

Put all the ingredients in a shaker and shake vigorously until frosted. Pour the liquid into a small cocktail glass, previously chilled with ice and then drained completely.

Rothman & Winter's *Crème de Violette is made from wild violet flowers growing in the Alps, added to a fine grain distillate. It results in a lightly sweet and very flowery mouthfeel. A perfect ingredient to wow guests!

Garnish with a Maraschino cherry.

Tuxedo

- 30 ml of Old Tom Gin
- 30 ml of dry vermouth
- 1/2 teaspoon of Maraschino Luxardo
- 1/4 teaspoon of absynthe
- 3 dashes of orange bitter

How to make

Put all the ingredients in a mixing glass with ice and mix well. Strain and pour into a previously chilled Martini glass.

Garnish with a Maraschino cherry and lemon zest.

Hanky Panky

- 45 ml of London Dry Gin
- 45 ml of red vermouth
- 7.5 ml of Fernet Branca

How to make

To prepare this cocktail pour all the ingredients into a mixing glass and stir with ice. Then pour into a chilled glass without ice and twist in a few drops of essential oils from an orange peel.

The Hanky Panky was created in 1903 by Ada Coleman, the first barwoman in history, at the historic Savoy bar in London. Ada invented this drink for Charles Hawtrey, a famous actor at the time and habitué of the hotel, who asked her for an energizing drink at the end of a work evening.

Casino

- 40 ml of Old Tom Gin
- 10 ml of Maraschino Luxardo
- 10 ml of fresh lemon juice
- 2 dashes of orange bitter

How to make

Put all the ingredients in a shaker filled with ice and shake until the surface is frosted. Strain the contents into a previously chilled cocktail glass.

Garnish with orange zest and a maraschino cherry.

Casino is a cocktail that comes from the Aviation: the Crème de Violette is replaced with orange bitter. The result is a less floral, but more citrusy and drier drink.

Martinez

- 45 ml of London Dry Gin
- 45 ml of red vermouth
- 1 bar spoon of Maraschino
- 2 dashes of Orange Bitter

How to make

Put all the ingredients directly into a mixing glass with ice and stir several times. Strain into a pre-chilled cocktail glass.

Finally garnish with a lemon zest.

The recipe is a masterpiece, a concentrate of the aromatic flavors of herbs and juniper that caress the palate under the sweet pull of maraschino. It can be said without hesitation that this is a cocktail suitable for all hours, whether as an aperitif or after dinner.

Gin Basil Smash

- 50 ml of Hendrick's Gin
- 25 ml of fresh lemon juice
- 12.5 ml of sugar syrup
- 8 fresh basil leaves

How to make

Put the basil leaves directly into the shaker and press them lightly. Then pour in all remaining ingredients with ice and shake until the metal is frosted.

Strain using fine-mesh strainer (double strain) and pour into an old-fashioned glass filled with ice. Garnish with a few basil leaves.

Created by Jörg Meyer in 2008 at Le Lion bar in Hamburg, Germany, the Gin Basil Smash is a refreshing summer cocktail with an herbaceous flavor and green, almost Midori-like color.

Paradise

- 30 ml of gin
- 20 ml of Apricot Brandy
- 15 ml of fresh orange juice

How to make

Put all the ingredients in a shaker with ice and shake well. Strain and pour contents into a previously chilled cocktail cup.

Serve without garnish. In some cases, orange is used, but in my opinion, it reinforces the citrus part of the drink too much. Use edible flowers instead.

Southside

- 60 ml of London Dry Gin
- 30 ml of fresh lemon juice
- 15 ml of sugar syrup
- 5/6 mint leaves
- Some drops of egg white

How to make

The Southside, probably in honor of the Chicago neighborhood, is a cool, sharp and refined cocktail that is very simple to make.

Start by chilling a cocktail glass by filling it with ice. Pour all the ingredients into a shaker with plenty of ice and shake vigorously for longer than normal to allow the egg white to incorporate air. Strain through a fine-mesh strainer (double-strain) into the emptied glass and garnish with a few mint leaves. If a fuller-bodied froth is desired on the surface, add a splash of soda.

Suffering Bastard

- 30 ml of cognac or brandy
- 30 ml of gin
- 15 ml of fresh lime juice
- 2 dashes of Angostura
- Top up with ginger beer (around 15 ml)

How to make

Put all the ingredients in a shaker except the ginger beer and shake with ice until the metal surface is frosted.

Strain and pour into a tall tumbler glass filled with ice or into the original Suffering Bastard Mug, a kind of ceramic cup that you can use to serve other "Tiki cocktails." Finish the drink with ginger beer and a gentle stir always from the bottom up.

Garnish with fresh mint, lime zest or a citrus slice to your liking.

The Suffering Bastard was invented by Joe Scialom in 1942. A chemistry graduate, he soon discovered how exciting it was to be a bartender, and so he became the head bartender at Shepheard's Hotel in Cairo. During World War II, the hotel was a privileged place for British officers and the press corps. Joe became very popular because of his talents: he spoke multiple languages, was very good at remembering names and faces, and especially the drinks his customers preferred.

One day, after hearing British officers complain about being hungover, Joe was inspired to create a hangover cure. He gathered ingredients that could be purchased locally and created the Suffering Bastard. The idea behind it was that if you wanted to get rid of a hangover, you had to get drunk again - today we know that is not the case.

Long Island Iced Tea

- 15 ml of vodka
- 15 ml of tequila
- 15 ml of white rum
- 15 ml of gin
- 15 ml of Cointreau
- 30 ml of fresh lemon juice
- 20 ml of sugar syrup
- Top with cola (about 20-30 ml)

How to make

Put ice and all the ingredients in a high tumbler or highball glass (capacity of around 350 ml) and stir with a bar spoon.

Alternatively, shake the ingredients except the cola and then pour into the glass. The result is the same, unless you add a few drops of egg white to create froth on the surface.

Garnish with a slice of lemon.

Incorrectly considered a boozy club drink due to many bartenders' inability to free pour the right measures of the ingredients at the same time. In this way, the quantity of alcohol is surely excessive.

Actually, the Long Island Iced Tea, if prepared following the recipe, has a total alcohol content of around 18%, in line with the majority of cocktails.

Do not exaggerate with the cola: the final color must be the same as iced tea, ergo its fame. Obviously invented in Long Island (New York) at the Oak Beach Inn in the 1970s by Robert Rosebud nicknamed "Butt", it was created for a Triple Sec-themed competition. Subsequently, teenagers started masking the cocktail as iced tea at parties.

(Author's note: the Long Island Iced Tea is not a true gin-based cocktail, rather a cocktail with many ingredients including gin. In any case, I wanted to include it in this book because, in my personal experience and not only, it represents one of the most ordered cocktails at bars for at least 30 years now. Nevertheless,

90% of the times it is prepared poorly, perhaps due to the unfortunate culture of drinking to get drunk and not to try new flavors).

ABOUT THE AUTHOR

Federico Illesi, nicknamed "Mr. Gin and Tonic" by his friends, was born in Bolzano, Italy, on 15 August 1984 and is a gin enthusiast just like you.

He has a bachelor's degree in biomedical engineering and is the head of a web services company. Always passionate about mixology and the art of good drinking, he cultivates his artistic vein to surprise friends and welcome guests. A passion for travel, along with curiosity and the search for new flavors have driven him to discover more. That is why in 2012 he obtained the bartender certification issued by A.I.B.E.S. (Associazione Italiana Barmen e Sostenitori), recognized worldwide by I.B.A. (International Bartenders Association), thanks to which he was finally able to get his ideas straight and avoid the most common mistakes of novices.

Since 2010, he also co-organizes a three-month summer event with evening entertainment, shows, discos and lounge bars.

The best suggestion among the many on the previous pages and that he will never tire of repeating? Use full ice cubes bought in handy bags: the ones from home, due to size and water impurity, will inevitably water down the drink!

Having reached this point, he would be happy to hear from you and receive your feedback on the book. Feel free to send an email to: federicoillesi@gmail.com

ACKNOWLEDGEMENTS

The making of this book has been possible thanks to the many people who have led me this far. I'll try to remember them all.

First of all, thanks to the professionals, who transmitted their knowledge to me and taught me the art of mixology.

Thanks to my friends and guests, who over the years - perhaps unknowingly - lent themselves to tasting my cocktails. I am grateful to all of them for their advice and feedback.

Thanks to Gian for supporting me, encouraging me and being the most difficult and attentive reader to convince!

Thanks to those who worked with me on the making of this book, reading its draft over and over again: Giusva, Bobo and Raniero.

Thanks to those who were able to give the book a cover, drawing heavily on the patience it takes with people like me, unaccustomed and not prone to being photographed: Rubina, Rodolfo and Mika.

Thanks to Thomaz for the help and material provided.

Thanks to the publisher and all the staff who collaborated to put it into print.

Finally, thank you to all the readers, who will spend some of their free time with me··· I hope to be a source of inspiration and pleasant entertainment for them.

INDEX